Charlotte Bergan Cioli

The Weekender

PARIS

Canal St Martin & Le Marais

COLLECTIVE SHORTS
by NHP PUBLISHING

“To Maman, who gave me the gift of language and my love of France,
and to Pappa, whose support made my dreams of Paris a reality.
Your love and guidance have shaped not only who I am, but also
the way I see the world through my lens.” – Charlotte

I was born a francophile. After all, my French mother raised me speaking her native tongue. Our kitchen was always fragrant with the smell of her cuisine, so *oui*, a love for France is in my blood. However, it wasn't until later that Paris became the center point of this affection. It all began in college, where I spent a semester in Paris. Then, a year working there remotely led me to a more permanent move, hauling with me my beloved vintage car, furniture, and boxes of books all the way from Florida. During those years, I had the greatest privilege of becoming acquainted with Paris and its streets, boutiques, and cafés.

Paris is charm, art, history, literature, romance, and beauty. Although our first thoughts may be *Eiffel Tower*, *Louvre*, *Notre Dame*, there is indeed so much more to my treasured Paris. As a photographer and artist, this city is my fountain-of-youth for inspiration. I embrace the clichés and am always happily strolling, humming, and of course, eating. Paris, the city of love (...of pains au chocolat.)

I've lived in the brutalist-area of *La Defense*. I've lived near the quiet and romantic *Parc Monceau*. I've lived in the bustling, boutique-filled *Marais*. But, my favorite home was on the *Canal Saint-Martin*. Somewhat nestled between *Montmartre and the Marais*, it's a neighborhood bursting with life, but away from the crowds of tourists. As soon as the temperatures rise, the canal is lined with Parisians who 'picole', sipping and snacking; turning this borough into a picture of Parisian hip, and one you simply cannot miss.

Weekender: Paris aims to take you through the city through a different itinerary than is typically offered. By skipping the sights thronged with tourists and introducing you to a very cool part of the city by way of my favorite streets, restaurants, and cafés. Come join me on a Thursday-through-Sunday weekend with both my camera and a croissant in hand, to explore the Canal Saint Martin and the Marais neighborhoods. If you know Paris, I hope it makes you smile with either familiarity or surprise. If you don't know Paris, I hope it inspires you to plan your first visit.

Charlotte Bergan Cioli

Cocktails - Vins

Thursday

VALERY, 2019
ELVIRA, 2021
BILLETS
Grandes
Lignes
achat
retrait
échange

Thursday 6:05 PM Arrival at Gare de L'Est

Neighborhood stroll before check-in

Thursday 6:20 PM

Porte Saint-Denis

Thursday 6:36 PM

LVDOVICO MAGNO

HOTEL GR

D AMOUR
COLONNE
SECHE

de ou par
MARCEL DUCHAMP
ou
RROSE SELAVY
ATELIER SEPTEMBER
PURPLE
LE MONDE DU SEXE
LES AILES DU DESIR
Fanny and Alexander
DOGTOOTH
MISFITS
AMERICAN YOUTH
POLANSKI
Bent

Thursday 7:04 PM

Pink literary dreams at Hotel Grand Amour

photographies

Grand Amour Restaurant Thursday 9:19 PM

GRAND
HOTEL
AMOUR

BAR

Thursday 10:37 PM

Pisco Sour at Book Bar

LE NAPOLEON

Tarte fine aux pommes

Friday

residence
kann

Friday 9:12 AM

Cappuccino at Residence Kann

10e ARR
RUE DE MARSEILLE
ATISSERIE
BOULANGERIE
BOU
FABRIC
EURRE FIN
PAIN A LA FARINE DE MEULE

RUE
YVES TOUDIC
ANGERIE
DU PAIN ET DES IDEES
34
ON TRADITIONNELLE
BOULANGERIE

Friday 9:35 AM

Du Pain et Des Idées for pains au chocolat

The turning bridge with Noisette　　Friday 10:13 AM

DANGER
ZONE
TECHNIQUE
ACCÈS
INTERDI.
AU PUBLIC

VEJA
GENERAL
STORE

Friday 11:15 AM

Pop into Veja General Store

...and the Central Commercial boutique

Friday 11:46 AM

Friday 12:30 PM

A farm-to-table lunch at Les Résistants

Friday 2:04 PM

Return to the Canal Saint-Martin

POLAR
DolceVita

Friday 2:18 PM

A sweet moment at JJ Hings

Antoine & Lili
Antoine & Lili
HOTEL

ZART
GALERIE
99 cats and a dog
GELATO AL NATURALE
QUAI VALMY
30

A new read at Artazar

Friday 3:10 PM

BEYOND CONSERVATIVE
crash
woman
BLANC
STUDY
Numéro
246
Végétal
System
beauty
FAMILY
ACHTUNG
the
gentlewoman
Griffé
DUST
BEHIND THE BLINDS
THE TRAVEL ALMANAC

Perfect porcelain at Alix D Reynis   Friday 4:04 PM

CAFÉ
SUCRE
ALIX D. REYNIS

RECETTE

ALIX D. REYNIS

New chef residency at Early June

Friday 6 PM

Saturday

Mamiche for a smörgåsbord of pastries

Saturday 9:14 AM

66

Saturday 10:08 AM

Timeless elegance behind teal doors.

CAFE THE

ROT VINTAGE
BISTROT VINTAGE
VINTAGE MATIERES
VINTAGE MATIERES
BISTROT BRILLANT
BISTROT BRILLANT
BRILLANT MATIERES

Saturday 10:44 AM

Choose colors for new cutlery at Sabres Paris

Musée Picasso

Saturday 11:26 AM

ROYAL BAR
CAFE & VIN
19
ROYAL BAR
CAFÉ-EXTRA
CHOCOLAT
LAIT
APÉRITIFS
FLAT WHITE
BLACK COFFEE
MATCHA LATTE
ICED COFFEE
CHAI, TEAS & MORE

Found some friends in Square Georges-Cain Saturday 1:28 PM

Saturday 1:44 PM

Light lunch at FIKA at the Institut Suédois

Wes Anderson moments at every corner

Saturday 2:20 PM

BISTROT
PARISIEN
GLACES
& SORBETS
Berthillon
VINS AU VERRE
FORMULE
DÉJEUNER & DÎNER
MARCHÉ
DU JOUR

LE BEAU TEMPS

ITION
CTOBRE
FOCUS
LE COSTUME AU ZÉNITH
CHECKLIST
LES INDISPENSABLES DE L'ÉTÉ
À PROPOS
OCTOBRE-EDITIONS.COM
PRINTEMPS / ÉTÉ 2024
CARTE POSTALE

Browsing the new collection at Octobre Editions

Saturday 3:03 PM

OCTOBRE-EDITIONS.COM

Welcome home!
To Grand Amour
André & Emmanuel

Saturday 4:02 PM

Back to the hotel to freshen up

Saturday 7:19 PM

Apéritif at Fabula

Saturday 9:04 PM

Restaurant Anne

CUISINE
BELLEVILLE
PORTRAITS DE LA NOUVELLE ARCHITECTURE
WORK
Malinowski
LES COMMANDOS
FAIRE FACE À LA MALADIE DE CHARCOT
PAULO COELHO
HENRI DE BRANCION
MARIE-JOSE JAUBERT
LA SYMPHONIE DES MONSTRES
MARC LEVY
RENE MANZOR
LES PARAS PERDUS
CONVOI 42
la méthode DUKAN
CUISINE DE LA SANTÉ
LA SANTÉ DEVANT SOI
Igor et Grichka Bogdanov
LE GOÛT DE VIEILLIR
manuel de Littérature
DUPUY
Tom Drury

Sunday

Sunday 9:22 AM

Heading to the metro

Sunday 10:15 AM

METRO
LE MONDE EN FAMILLE

Tickets
Sortie
1 place de la République
2 r. du Temple
3 av. de la République
4 r. du Fbg du Temple

Services
Sortie
1 place de la République
2 r. du Temple
3 av. de la République
4 r. du Fbg du Temple

Chairs of Parisian cafés by the Seine

Sunday 11:01 AM

Sunday 12:17 PM

Péniche Marcounet for lunch

French essentials at Laurent Dubois   Sunday 1:47 PM

Au Revoir Paris

Sunday 2:40 PM

GARE DE L'EST
SNCF

The Weekender

PARIS

Canal St Martin & Le Marais

Published by New Heroes & Pioneers
Photography and text: Charlotte Bergan Cioli
Creative Direction: Francois Le Bled
Series Book Design: Daniel Zachrisson
Edition Book Design: Lilith Onyett
Models: Alessandro Cioli, Dahlia Subasi & Franklin Cioli

Print and bound by BALTO print (Lithuania)
Legal deposit November 2024
ISBN 9789198656589

MIX
Paper | Supporting responsible forestry
FSC® C107574
www.fsc.org

"With a big merci to François Le Bled, Cheyne Tillier-Daly, Dahlia Subasi, and my husband, Alessandro Cioli"
Charlotte Bergan Cioli

Hotel Grand Amour - grandamour.hotelamourparis.fr
Residence Kann - kanndesign.com
Du Pain et Des Idées -dupainetdesidees.com
Centre Commercial - centrecommercial.cc
Veja General Store - veja-store.com/en_eu/store-general-store
Les Résistants - lesresistants.fr
JJ Hings Ice Cream - instagram.com/jjhings
Artazar Librairie - artazart.com
Early June - early-june.fr
Mamiche - mamiche.fr
Musée Picasso - museepicassoparis.fr
Café FIKA - paris.si.se/en/our-offer/cafe-fika
Alix D Reynis - alixdreynis.com
Sabres Paris - sabre-paris.com
Octobre Editions - octobre-editions.com
Fabula - fabula.paris
Restaurant Anne - en.pavillon-de-la-reine.com/restaurant-bar
5 Pailles - 5pailles.com
Fromages Laurent Dubois - fromageslaurentdubois.fr
Péniche Marcounet - peniche-marcounet.fr

COLLECTIVE SHORTS
by NHP PUBLISHING

GOLD'S GYM GUIDE TO FITNESS

TAKE THE CARDIO CHALLENGE

THE EXPERTS AT GOLD'S GYM

Enslow Publishing
101 W. 23rd Street
Suite 240
New York, NY 10011
USA
enslow.com

This edition published in 2019 by Enslow Publishing, LLC.
101 W. 23rd Street, Suite 240, New York, NY 10011

Cataloging-in-Publication Data

Names: The experts at Gold's Gym.
Title: Take the cardio challenge / The experts at Gold's Gym.
Description: New York : Enslow Publishing, 2019.
| Series: Gold's Gym guide to fitness | Includes glossary and index.
Identifiers: ISBN 9781978506855 (pbk.) | ISBN 9781978506572 (library bound)
| ISBN 9781978506862 (6-pack)
Subjects: LCSH: Cardiovascular fitness—Juvenile literature. | Aerobic exercises—Juvenile literature.
| Physical fitness—Juvenile literature.
Classification: LCC RA645.C34 O949 2019 | DDC 616.1/071—dc23

Printed in the United States of America

To Our Readers: We have done our best to make sure all website addresses in this book were active and appropriate when we went to press. However, the author and the publisher have no control over and assume no liability for the material available on those websites or on any websites they may link to. Any comments or suggestions can be sent by e-mail to customerservice@enslow.com.

Photo credits: All Gold's Glow Photography courtesy of Gold's Gym, with the following exceptions: ICON Health and Fitness (p. 6 top, 26 top); United Legwear & Apparel Co. (p. 14 bottom right).

All other photos courtesy of Shutterstock.com: AM-STUDiO (p. 24 top); v.s.anandhakrishna (p. 14 bottom left); Marcin Balcerzak (p. 16 above); Connel (p. 32); djgis (p. 40); Dragon Images (p. 20–21); Dudarev Mikhail (p. 25); Dana E. Fry (p. 44); Sumate Gulabutdee (p. 31 bottom); lassedesignen (p. 14 top); Maridav (p. 16 below); mimagephotography (p. 15 top); Mooshny (p. 18 bottom); ostill (p. 41); Oleksiy Rezin (p. 30–31); Stefan Schurr (p. 17); swinner (p. 24); Syda Productions (p. 39 top); Uber Images (p. 7); wavebreakmedia (p. 45); Yuriy Rudyy (p. 22 bottom).

All exercise instructional illustrations by Remie Geoffroi.

All anatomical illustrations by design36/Shutterstock.com, except p. 18 top by Sebastian Kaulitzki/ Shutterstock.com.

All other illustrations courtesy of Shutterstock.com: pking4th icon in upper right corner headings.

CONTENTS

INTRODUCTION

Cardiovascular training—any activity that raises your heart rate and increases the circulation of blood—can speed up metabolism, improve stamina, and strengthen both the heart and lungs. As such, cardio should be considered a necessary component of a balanced fitness regimen.

KNOW YOUR CARDIO

There are various forms of cardiovascular exercise—biking, walking, running, rowing, aerobics, dancing, swimming, martial arts, and boxing, among many others—and different methods for performing them that offer specific benefits. When creating a cardio routine, consult with a trainer to make sure your plan is providing the benefits you seek.

UNDERSTAND THE BENEFITS

Although some forms of cardio are slightly more effective for weight loss, all will efficiently burn calories. More moderate methods of cardio can also decrease workout recovery time—after an intense session with weights, a relaxed stint on the treadmill will help eliminate the by-products created by your body. Eventually you might want to investigate advanced forms of cardio, such as interval training, tempo training, and HIIT sprints.

The benefits of cardio workouts are manifold. In addition to weight loss and a stronger heart and lungs, you will increase your bone density, gain more energy, develop better sleep habits, lower your stress levels, find temporary relief of depression and anxiety, reduce risk of heart disease and some types of cancer, manage your diabetes by utilizing more glucose, and increase your confidence. You will also be setting a good example for others in your family and circle of friends by staying active.

BUILD YOUR PROGRAM

You'll hear a lot of opinions about how much cardio to include in your regimen; a commonly accepted guideline suggests 30 minutes of moderate cardio five days a week or 20 minutes of more intense exercise three days a week. To achieve weight loss, you might find that you need as much as 60 to 90 minutes per session.

TOOLS of the TRADE

TACKLE THE TREADMILL

The treadmill is a piece of equipment used for walking or running in place. It consists of a wide, conveyor-belt footbed, and a sturdy frame with a front stability brace topped by a console. The tread, which offers different levels of resistance, can be self-propelled or, in more expensive models, motorized. The console of electronic models typically features a lit display with different speed and terrain settings, a timer, and a mileage counter. Some even have programs that monitor calories burned and heart rate, as well as touch-screen access to TV, the internet, popular fitness apps, and interactive courses.

Over time, this mainstay of the commercial gym has become one of the most valued additions to the home gym. Advantages of the treadmill include the ability to complete your cardio session no matter the weather; a cushioned tread that is easier on the feet and legs than running on a hard roadbed, incline settings that allow you to run "uphill" for additional toning benefits, and rate settings that allow you to maintain a steady pace or choose variable speeds. Look for models like the Gold's Gym Trainer 430i, which is iFit Bluetooth Smart Enabled, iPod compatible, and combines quick speed with incline control. Many users also watch TV or DVDs while on the treadmill, turning a once-sedentary activity into a healthy workout.

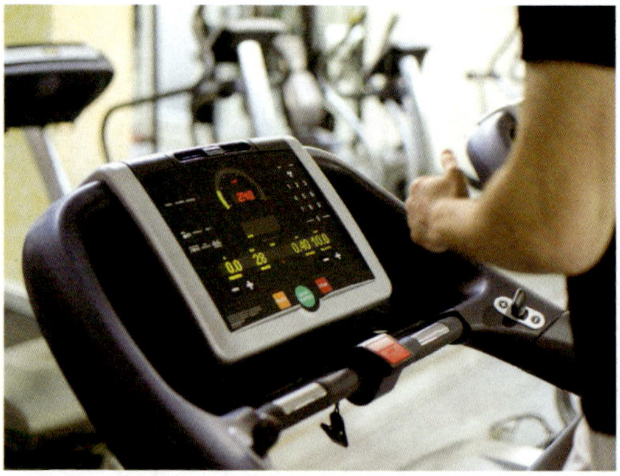

MAKE THE MOST OF YOUR TREADMILL WORKOUT

The treadmill can offer a comprehensive cardio workout to gym-goers of all levels, especially if you follow these suggestions.

WARM UP PROPERLY Never just climb onto the machine and kick it into high gear. A typical session would be warming up first with three minutes of walking. Follow with three minutes of jogging and then three sets of 20-second speed sprints with 40 seconds of recovery in between.

PLACE GEAR NEARBY The point of the treadmill—or any cardio machine—is to exert yourself until you sweat, so keep a hand towel on the console, and pat yourself dry as needed. A water bottle that opens with one hand is a great way to stay hydrated without stopping to fiddle with a screw cap.

PAY ATTENTION TO CADENCE There are two ways to run faster—lengthening your stride or upping the number of smaller strides, thus increasing cadence. The treadmill is perfect for the latter: you have a timer in front of you, and you can hear your foot strike the tread in order to find the sweet spot, which should be fairly quiet. Count the strikes of one foot in 15 seconds, and multiply times 4. You should be aiming for 90 beats per foot per minute.

UP THE INCLINE Because, by many accounts, running on a treadmill actually feels similar to running slightly downhill, keep the incline on your machine set to 1 percent to compensate.

RECOVER SLOWLY The general rule of thumb for ending your session is to cool down one minute for every mile run, so a five-mile (8 km) workout requires an easy-paced five-minute walk.

SET YOUR TREADMILL ON AN INCLINE GRADE

Uphill workouts are among the best exercises you can do because they provide a high-intensity cardio session while also having a low impact on your joints. Recent studies have shown that incline work—even walking up steep angles—has a wide variety of benefits. Your sessions, whether walking or running, have the potential to build strength and power, burn fat, tone muscle, and increase the stroke volume of your heart, while at the same time strengthening the lower back, glutes, quads, hamstrings, and calves. This machine even speeds up the pace at which your brain sends messages to your muscles.

Gold's Gym Fitness Institute member Robert Reames configured these three workouts that combine walking and running. A treadmill is the best place for hill workouts because it removes the most troublesome aspect: the downhill. Most hill-related injuries actually occur on the downslope—the reverse incline adds a gravity-induced load. So the treadmill has all the great uphill benefit with none of the, well, downside of the downhill.

As a general guide, you should set the treadmill incline between a 4- and 10-percent grade, and set your sprint speed from 7.5 to 10 miles per hour (12–16 kpm). Focus on pushing yourself, but be sure to maintain good posture, keeping your hips, shoulders, and neck relaxed. Add one of these workouts to your current routine or pair them up for even more intensity.

THE 10-MINUTE WORKOUT

- 3 minutes warm-up
- 1.5 minutes high-incline power walk
- 1 minute rest interval
- 1.5 minutes sprint
- 3 minutes cool-down

THE 15-MINUTE WORKOUT

- 2 minutes slow warm-up
- 1 minute moderate warm-up
- 1.5 minutes high-incline power walk
- 1.5 minutes high-incline sprint
- 3 minutes rest interval
- 1.5 minutes high-incline power walk
- 1.5 minute high-incline sprint
- 2 minutes moderate cool-down
- 1 minute slow cool-down

THE 20-MINUTE WORKOUT

- 2 minutes slow warm-up
- 2 minutes moderate warm-up
- 2 minutes high-incline power walk
- 2 minutes rest interval
- 2 minutes high-incline sprint
- 2 minutes rest interval
- 2 minutes high-incline power walk
- 2 minutes rest interval
- 2 minutes cool-down on flat grade
- 2 minutes cool-down interval on flat grade

OVERCOME OBSTACLES

Many competitive runners and recreational joggers who run outdoors are resistant to the treadmill at first. Here are some challenges they've noted, and how to overcome them.

SIZE The treadmill is not a portable piece of equipment that can be folded up and stored under a bed. So, if you have a small apartment, maybe keep your treadmill sessions to the gym.

VARIETY If you're used to running outdoors in all kinds of weather, through varied scenery, running in place can mean a real adjustment. This might mean it's time to set up the DVD player or add thumping new tunes to your iPod. Runners who relish the ever-changing scenery of the urban or rural landscape tend to find the treadmill's limited vistas lack appeal and offer little sense of adventure.

PACING If you stay at one pace for an entire workout, you can feel unbalanced. Make use of the many options for interval training to mix things up, varying your pace and incline to better mimic an outdoor workout.

GAIT Some treadmill users who return to outdoor running feel like they've developed a short, upright, bouncy gait—possibly as a result of having no wind resistance indoors. This is another case where mixing up speed and incline can help.

COMPETITION If you're training for serious track and field events, the treadmill isn't the optimal training idea. You'll probably want to look for a good indoor or outdoor track.

GET YOUR HEART PUMPING

Your heart is a muscle, and it benefits from exercises that give it a workout and make it strong, just like any other muscle in your body. By asking the heart to pump at a faster rate on a regular basis, you can get it into shape and keep it healthy. If you find you are winded just from performing simple tasks like walking up the stairs or lifting a basket of laundry, you're probably neglecting to work your heart muscle—and that's something to remedy. Cardiovascular disease can affect anyone, and heart health is not to be taken lightly. The good news is that finding solutions is easy—anything aerobic that gets you moving and elevates your heart rate—like walking briskly, jumping rope, or riding a bike—will work. You might have to start slow, but before long you can tackle exhilarating cycling workouts or compete in charity runs.

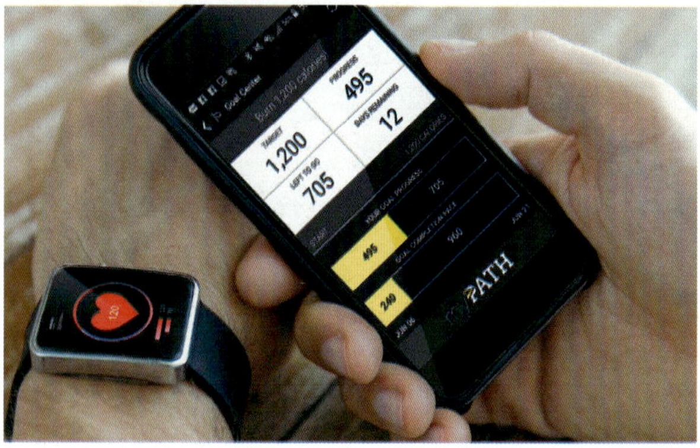

MONITOR YOUR HEART

During any taxing exercise, it's important to watch your heart rate and record your progress. A heart rate monitor (HRM) will track your pulse, and it will also help you figure out when you're at maximum exertion levels, will track calories burned, and will let you know if you hit fat-burning zones. It's a great tool regardless of your fitness level, and dependable models can be purchased for as little as $35.

CHEST STRAP HRMs These include a wireless sensor on a chest strap that detects your pulse electronically and then sends that data to a wrist receiver that displays your heart rate. Basic chest-strap HRMs will also time your workout and give you continuous, average, high, and low heart-rate data.

STRAPLESS HRMs A sensor in the wrist unit's band detects your pulse. You may find strapless HRMs more comfortable, but they tend to be less accurate than chest-strap HRMs, and they don't typically sync with speed and distance sensors.

GET IN THE ZONE

Determining the optimal heart-rate target zone for your specific goal is essential. The target zone is the percentage range you will aim for and is based on your maximum heart rate (MHR). The simplest calculation is: MHR = 220 minus your age. A more precise figure is 216 minus 93% of your age for men and 200 minus 67% of your age for women. There are four zones. The highest, or VO_2 Max, enhances speed, but for short bursts only because the muscle groups subject to this much effort will soon become deprived of oxygen.

ENDURANCE (60 TO 70 PERCENT) This range works for endurance and weight loss and develops cardio and muscular efficiency. In this zone, your body burns stored fat as fuel.

AEROBIC (70 TO 80 PERCENT) This range is ideal for overall cardio fitness, weight management, and muscle strength. In this zone, your body burns mostly fat and carbs.

ANAEROBIC (80 TO 90 PERCENT) This is the range for interval workouts or consistent speed. You will breathe heavily and feel your muscles tire out in this zone, but you'll increase lung capacity and get other long-term benefits.

THINK *about it*

To take your own pulse, place two fingers between the bone and the tendon over the radial artery, on the thumb side of your wrist. Count the number of beats for 15 seconds, and multiply by four.

HEART RATE MONITOR APPS

You have so many options for tracking your heart rate, from high-tech systems with wireless heart rate monitors that strap to your chest and connect with your phone to apps that use your phone's flash to take readings. iRunXtreme and Heart Rate Monitor allow you to monitor your heart rate using your iPhone microphone, while iHeart measures your heart rate as you hold onto your iPhone. Hcalc, also available for your iPhone, makes it easy to track your heart rate and target a specific range for your workouts. For Android users, Instant Heart Rate, Runtastic Heart Rate, and Cardiograph are ranked among the best.

- *Cardio Buddy*
- *Cardiograph*
- *Cardiio*
- *Hcalc*
- *Heart Rate Monitor*
- *iHeart*
- *Instant Heart Rate*
- *iRunXtreme*
- *MotionX247*
- *Runtastic Heart Rate*

TRACK YOUR ACTION

Wearable devices that allow you to track your mileage, intensity levels, heart rate, and more, while you run, walk, bike, swim, or perform other forms of cardio exercise are a firm part of the fitness scene. These trackers can also act as motivators, encouraging you to keep moving and meet your daily goals.

The simplest device is a basic pedometer, a portable electronic or electromechanical device that you can clip on or attach to a lanyard so that it counts the steps you take each day by detecting the motion of your hands or hips. Pedometer functionality can also be introduced to smartphones, iPods, and MP3 players that have integrated accelerometers.

The current stars of the fitness world are the various wearable activity monitors ("wearables") that count steps and may display distance traveled, goals met, calories burned, and the intensity of the workout. When worn in an armband at night, certain versions measure the length and quality of your sleep; some can even wake you with a vibrating alarm. Most wearables connect to your computer via USB, where your data is automatically uploaded and displayed on a profile web page. Depending on the manufacturer, some versions can access a wide range of fitness apps. Microsoft and Apple both have their own devices; popular platform-agnostic brands include Fitbit, Garmin, and Polar. Certain devices are tailored to specific activities such as swimming or cycling, so do some online research to see which device will best suit your needs.

AMP UP YOUR ENDURANCE

Many people who work out regularly complain that they eventually become fatigued while exercising or even while doing chores at home. The trick to improving endurance and staying power is to add strength moves to your cardio workout—cardio will make you aerobically fit, while strength training will propel you through demanding workouts. If you are a runner, adding muscle will also help absorb the impact of your feet hitting the ground that would otherwise stress your joints. Here are some strength-boosting suggestions.

COMBINE STRENGTH DAYS WITH CARDIO DAYS Do bench presses and pull-ups followed by a speedy circuit of the track, or jump rope for a minute, and then do a series of squats, overhead presses, and crunches.

REDUCE YOUR REST Give yourself only a minimal break or no break at all between sets. Perform three sets of 10 back-to-back exercises such as pull-ups, squats, push-ups, and crunches. By the end, you should be sweating and your muscles should be burning.

OPT FOR COMPOUND MOVEMENTS Get more bang for your buck with exercises that use more than one joint—such as squats, step-ups, pull-ups—instead of isolated movements.

ADD EXPLOSIVES Incorporating explosive plyometric movements, like box jumps and jumping knee tucks, into your session will soon have you moving faster—and longer.

CHANGE YOUR ROUTINE Your body will adapt to a particular workout after only two weeks, so it's important to move your muscles in a different way by incorporating new activities into old routines—in other words, keeping your body guessing. Runners could try martial arts disciplines; cyclists might move onto the stair climber machine.

CHECK OUT HYBRIDS These exercises take two separate movements and combine them—a squat with an overhead press, a jumping pull-up, or a lunge with bicep curls are some examples. The more muscles you engage, the more your heart is stimulated, increasing your stamina.

SPIKE YOUR METABOLISM

In addition to working your heart, cardio exercise can also increase the rate of various other processes in the body, known as your metabolism. The more intense your cardio session, the more you'll notice an uptick in your metabolic rate. The experts at Gold's Gym offer several ways you can amp up your metabolism, which means you'll have an easier time maintaining your weight—or shedding excess pounds.

JETTISON THE STRESS Stress is a well-known cause of midriff and belly weight. Relaxation therapy, like yoga, can lower stress levels and bring back your metabolic oomph.

GET QUALITY SLEEP People who sleep at odd hours or who don't get enough sleep can stress their bodies and disrupt their metabolism. Try to maintain a consistent sleep schedule with at least eight hours nightly.

FOCUS ON NUTRITION If you eat a protein along with a fiber, some carbohydrates, and a good fat, you're keeping your insulin levels steady, so you're burning fat instead of storing fat. Eating protein at every meal is also key—it builds muscle, and more muscle leads to higher metabolic rates.

SPICE IT UP Hot, spicy seasonings, such as cayenne pepper or turmeric, will jump-start your metabolism. Add them to meat and fish rubs, egg dishes, soups, stews, and salad dressings.

DRINK EIGHT GLASSES Water, which is the foundation of so many chemical reactions in the body, is necessary for proper metabolic functions. Drinking green tea and coffee can also boost metabolism.

LEARN YOUR CARDIO OPTIONS

Determining the best cardio exercises to include in your routine depends on many factors. Do you like doing cardio in the gym, or would you prefer to take it outside? Other than the cardio benefits, are you also looking to lose weight or tone muscle? The chart below can serve as a basic guide, indicating how many calories some typical exercises and cardio machines burn and listing their main health benefits. The calories burned are based on a person of average weight.

MODALITY	CALORIES BURNED	BENEFITS
WALKING	200/hour moderate pace	Heart, lungs, weight control, blood pressure, bones and muscles, balance and coordination
RUNNING	270/half hour at 10 MPH	Heart, lungs, muscle mass, weight control, blood pressure, and reduces stress
CYCLING	650/hour moderate pace	Heart, lungs, muscle strength and tone, balance and coordination, mental health, and low impact
ROWING	200/half hour moderate pace	Heart, lungs, muscle tone, reduced strain on back and joints, weight loss, and reduces stress
SWIMMING	250/half-hour slow freestyle	Heart, lungs, muscle strength, weight maintenance, and low impact
AEROBICS	195/half hour moderate pace	Heart, respiration efficiency, improves blood volume and delivery to muscles
STAIR CLIMBER	180/half hour moderate pace	Heart, lungs, muscles, slows bone loss, and low impact
TREADMILL	350/half hour moderate-pace jog	Heart, lungs, muscle tone, weight loss, insulin control, and reduces stress
ELLIPTICAL	330/half hour moderate pace	Heart, lungs, weight control, blood pressure, bones and muscles, balance and coordination, and low impact

GO FOR A RUN

Running and jogging are some of the most popular recreational sports in the world. This is not surprising, because scientists believe that our bodies evolved, quite literally, to run. Today, people run for a variety of reasons—to lose weight, lower blood pressure, and strengthen the heart, as a way to tone the body, and to increase fitness and endurance for a specific sport. The benefits are impressive: running burns an average of 135 to 150 calories per mile, increases lean body mass and bone density, regulates cholesterol, and improves your psychological state by boosting endorphins.

Running allows great freedom—you can run at any time of day or night and find a track, trail, or sidewalk in most places. And because you don't need health club memberships or sports trainers, it is also relatively low-cost. A good pair of running shoes, some comfortable clothing, and a portable water bottle, and you're good to go. Still, as is the case with any athletic discipline, there is a right—and a wrong—way to run.

CHOOSE THE PROPER SNEAKERS

As a runner, buying a pair of quality shoes will be your main expense. Because these shoes are meant to support your feet, calves, and knees, and protect your body from injury, their workmanship and fit count big time. If possible, get measured at a store that specializes in sports footwear. The clerk should determine your arch shape—if you are flat-footed, or if you have a tendency to over- or underpronate the foot—and then suggest shoes that compensate. This person should also factor in your level of experience, how much you intend to run, and your average pace. Once you've gotten the proper shoes, break them in slowly. And bear in mind that most running shoes will last between 300 to 500 miles (500–800 km).

GET THE SUPPORT YOU NEED

Many female runners need added bust support in the form of a sports bra that minimizes movement but is not uncomfortably restrictive. Quality bras should be relatively seam-free, offer comfort, uplift, and have nonslip straps. They are typically made of a wicking synthetic fabric and come in sporty colors. If your sports bras are no longer doing the job, try wearing two at a time until you can find a workable replacement.

START OUT SLOW

All runners need to prepare for their sessions with a warm up, following each run with a similar cool-down period. If you are new to running, start out slowly so that your body can adjust to the new demands you'll be placing on it. Begin your regimen by walking 20 minutes three times a week. The second week, combine walking and running for 20 minutes over three nonconsecutive days. Pace yourself by alternating walking with running. During the third week, jog or run for 20 minutes for three nonconsecutive days. (A jog is trotting at a leisurely pace.) Pause or walk if you need to—but never stop moving. During subsequent weeks, gradually increase the duration, intensity, and frequency of your runs. If your body complains that you're doing too much, ease back.

GYM *etiquette*

FIND YOUR LANE

There are protocols to running on any track, but it is more critical to follow these rules on narrower, more confining indoor tracks. Faster runners traditionally keep to the inside track, and slower runners stay in the middle lanes, with walkers on the far outside. If two running buddies are moving abreast and hear someone coming from behind, the inner one should shift to the slower lane behind his or her friend. And if you are passing someone, call out "On your right!" to signal that you are approaching. Note that in most gyms the track direction changes every other day.

UNDERSTAND THE TERRAIN

When you are running on different surfaces, your body reacts to the impact in different ways. Switching surfaces is actually a smart tactic to strengthen your internal frame and lower the risk of repetitive-strain injuries and muscle imbalances.

GRASS One of the best surfaces to run on, grass is soft, low-impact, and great for speed work. It is often uneven, however, and long grass may hide animal holes, rocks, or other hazards. Grass also turns slippery when wet.

WOODLAND TRAILS Many parks and state forests offer well-maintained, level trails with soft, well-drained peat or wood chips underfoot. These materials are easy on the legs, and will help you develop your muscles and joints. Watch out for tree roots or slippery mud.

DIRT TRAILS The consistency of dirt can range from dry, sandy soil to moist, clay earth. Dry dirt is usually medium to soft underfoot, reducing your risk of training injuries and the impact of downhill runs. Avoid dirt trails in wet weather.

SYNTHETIC TRACK Outdoor tracks, with their flat, forgiving surfaces, are ideal for speed work and interval training. Tracks can become boring, however, and they may increase your risk of injury if you land hard on your inside leg, or if you roll your ankle and turn your foot outward negotiating the curves.

ASPHALT This common paving material is one of the fastest surfaces for running. It provides an even footing that will not stress your Achilles tendon. Unfortunately, there are traffic, potholes, and a hard unyielding surface to contend with.

SAND Flat and firm sand offers a forgiving, low-impact surface. Running up and down sand dunes provides effective resistance training, strengthening the legs. Running in soft sand gives your calf muscles a good workout, yet is easy on your joints. It also allows you to shed your shoes and go barefoot, which many experts believe is the best way to run.

CONCRETE City runners quickly learn to handle concrete, which is often the only surface available for them. It is the hardest material to run on and takes a toll on the legs; it also comes with curbs, pedestrians, and traffic signals.

KNOW WHY YOU FEEL SO GOOD

As you perform your regular running workout, jogging on the pavement or sprinting along a trail, you may find yourself overcome by a glowing sense of euphoria—this is the celebrated "runner's high" that track and field athletes and marathoners frequently experience. Running, along with other cardiovascular exercise, can actually change your hormonal profile, triggering the release of "feel good" hormones, such as endorphins. These can elevate your mood, ease depression, and block pain. Serotonin, another pleasure-producing chemical, works with endorphins to make exercise almost addictive; it also provides energy and promotes clear thinking. Another benefit of cardio: other released hormones, like peptide YY, can act as appetite suppressants.

RUNNING APPS

Runners have access to a wide range of multifunction apps to monitor their workouts and nutrition, map their routes, and track their progress. RunKeeper, MapMyRun, Fitbit, Runtastic, and Pact all share info; Zombies Run doesn't share, but it's a great motivator for the reluctant runner. Competitive runners should check out RaceJoy or iRace, or download Motigo so that friends and family can cheer you on, or Strava to join in challenges.

- *Couch to 5K*
- *Endomondo*
- *iRace*
- *MapMyRun*
- *Motigo*
- *Pacejamek*
- *Pact*
- *RaceJoy*
- *RunKeeper*
- *Runtastic*
- *SmartRunner*
- *Strava*
- *Wahoo*
- *Zombies Run*

STAY HYDRATED FOR RUNNING

Keeping the body hydrated is paramount for runners. In addition to the water you carry on the trail, try the following problem solvers before or after your run.

SLUGGISHNESS Drink a cup of green tea 20 to 30 minutes before you set out. The caffeine will power you and pep you up, and the antioxidants may increase endurance.

SIDE STITCH Coconut water contains 15 times more cramp-preventing potassium than sports drinks. Drink eight ounces (240 ml) before or during your run.

SORENESS To prevent next-day aches and pain, try chocolate milk with its perfect ratio of carbs to protein and high calcium content. Drink a cup 30 minutes after a long run.

EXCESS SWEAT Sports drinks replenish sugars and electrolytes lost by sweating. Find one with no artificial colors, flavors, or preservatives, and sip six ounces (175 ml) every 15 minutes.

COMPETE ON THE STREET

Once you feel comfortable running over distances, you should consider entering an organized event. Anyone, at any age, can race if they are willing to compete—plus, race training is a great motivator that can boost your running to the next level. First, determine what race type appeals to you—there are short charity and fun runs, themed runs, trail races, team obstacle races, qualifying runs, marathons, and half marathons. You also need to consider the terrain (if you run on flat urban streets, a hilly off-road race is likely not for you), how far you are willing to travel, the climate and temperatures you prefer, and what kind of experience you hope to gain. The cost of races vary: charity races may require you to find sponsorship; other races may charge a fee—from as low as $5 to $20 for a 5K to hundreds for a marathon.

PREPARE TO RACE

If you are considering competitive running, Team USA duathlete Lindsey Torgerson has some tips for distance runners that can also be applied to other types of racing.

GIVE YOURSELF TIME Plan for a 5K race at least 6 to 8 weeks out—12 to 14 weeks for a half marathon—but don't rush training, because it can cause injury. Start by running three days a week: ideally a slow long-distance run, a tempo run, and a speed/interval training day.

GET STRONG Strength training is critical to becoming a strong, healthy runner. Incorporate two to three strength-training sessions per week.

TAKE TIME OUT If you are feeling tired, hungrier than usual, and stiff or sore, take the day off to allow your body to recover.

CHECK YOURSELF Ask a friend to film you running, then assess your foot strike and upper-body movements. If you are heel striking, this can cause lower back, hip, and knee issues. Midfoot should be your initial contact with the pavement, and your elbows should be sliding close to your sides, hands relaxed.

RUN OUTSIDE Do at least one of your weekly training runs outside on the street. You will be running your race outside, and you need to be comfortable on pavement.

FIND YOUR FUEL You should usually eat one hour before any physical activity. Use your training weeks to determine your best pre- and post-run fuels.

KNOW YOUR... HIP FLEXORS

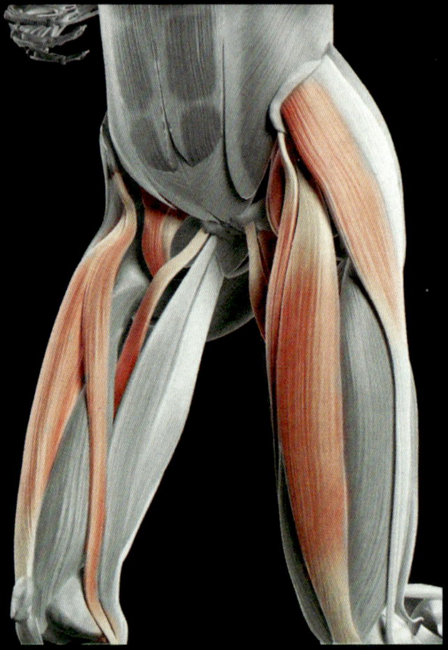

The hip flexors are a powerful group of muscles that you rely on whenever you walk, jog or sprint. These muscles are attached to the hip joint to allow your knee to pull upward. The hip itself is a large ball-and-socket joint that joins many ligaments, tendons, and muscles. The main hip flexor is the iliopsoas group, which consists of two muscles: the psoas and the iliac. These deep, hidden muscles are crucial to good posture, helping to stabilize your spine. Weak iliopsoas muscles may lead to lower-back and pelvic pain (running commonly triggers hip flexor problems). The rectus femoris and the sartorius are the other two major hip flexors. The sartorius aids in the flexion of your knee and hip and the rotation of your thigh and tibia bone. The rectus femoris—one of the four quadriceps muscles—is the only muscle that crosses over the hip joint, which enables it to work as both a hip flexor and a knee extender. Other hip flexors are the tensor fasciae latae, along your outer thigh, and the gracilis, pectineus, adductor longus, and adductor brevis on the inner thigh. At the back is the adductor magnus, which acts as a hip extensor.

WARM UP AND COOL DOWN

It may seem as simple as dragging yourself out of bed and hitting the pavement, but a smart running regimen means warming up before you sprint at top speed and cooling down at the end of your run. Follow these tips to run at your best and avoid possible injury.

WALK BEFORE YOU RUN Start off with a gentle walk for a few minutes to ease your body into the intense workout to come. Walking will get the range of motion of your muscles, tendons, and joints up to speed and raise the temperature of your muscles and core, increasing the blood flow to your running muscles.

PICK UP YOUR PACE To transition from walking to running mode, move into a slow jog for two minutes. Then gradually pick up your pace, accelerating your speed over 200 to 300 feet (60–100 m), and then just as gradually decelerate. Next, walk a bit more, shaking out your legs for a couple of minutes. Repeat the whole sequence in the opposite direction.

STRETCH YOUR RUNNING MUSCLES Forget static, fixed stretches—although once a regular part of a running regimen, they can actually make you more susceptible to injury. Instead, perform a series of dynamic stretches. These controlled movements improve range of motion, loosen up muscles, and increase your heart rate, body temperature, and blood flow. Focus on dynamic stretches aimed at your running muscles, like your legs, glutes, and hip flexors.

COOL YOURSELF DOWN You may be tempted to just flop into a chair, but a proper cool-down will bring your body back to a resting state, just as the warm-up brought it to an active state. A proper cool-down should gently slow your elevated heart rate and help clear your muscles of metabolic waste. To cool-down, drop to a jog and then a walk. Your next step is to perform a series of dynamic stretches—you can march or skip with high knees and shuffle with straight legs, for example, or perform the same kind of stretches you did for your warm-up.

TARGETED workout

GET READY TO RUN

Dynamic stretches will warm your muscles and prepare them for a run. There are many dynamic stretches, but be sure to include in your warm-up those that target key running muscle groups: the ones that control flexion and extension of the legs and lateral movements. Always include exercises that warm up your hips—this is where the hip flexors, quads, and hamstrings come together.

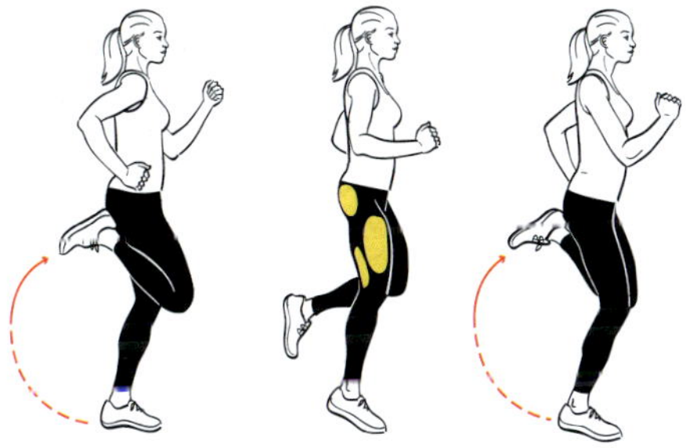

A **BUTT KICKS** Butt kicks will warm up the muscles in your legs and increase your core body temperature. Start slowly, and work up to a faster speed.

HOW Stand tall with a tight core and flat back, and bring your left foot back and up to your glutes. Return your foot to the ground, and repeat with the right. Continue alternating legs, keeping your knees slightly bent at all times and pumping your arms to run in place for two minutes.

B **PLYO LUNGE** This is a great plyometric move to warm up your entire lower body—including the quadriceps, glutes, hamstrings, and calves—and activate the stabilizer muscles in your legs and hips.

HOW Stand in a wide lunge with your right leg forward and your arms at your sides. Bend your knees, and then explode upward, switching your legs midair so that you land with your left leg forward and right foot back. Land softly, compressing right into another lunge, and then alternate sides for 10 reps.

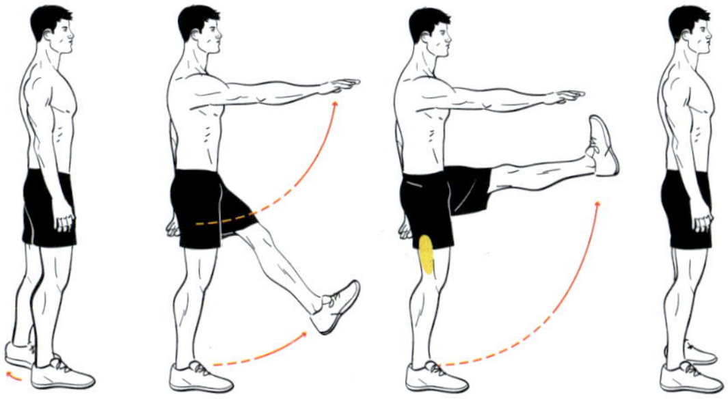

C **MONSTER WALK** This walking exercise will stretch your hamstrings.

HOW While walking a distance of 20 yards (18.2 m), kick one leg up in the air to a comfortable height while trying to touch the toe with the opposite arm. Repeat for the full distance, alternating legs and arms.

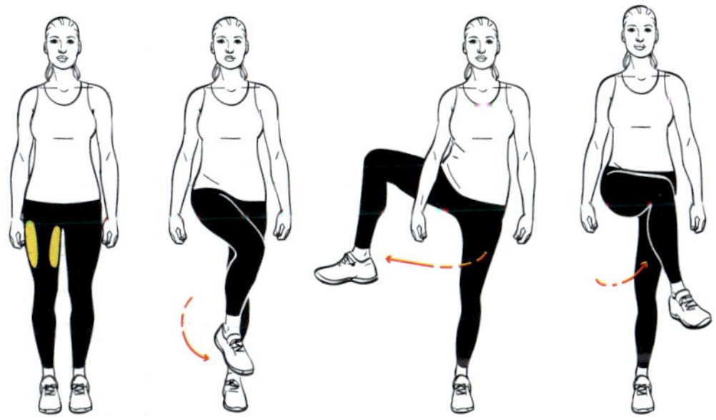

D **OPEN AND CLOSE THE GATE** This move combines hip adduction and abduction to warm up your hip flexors and groin muscles.

HOW Walking a distance of 20 yards (18.2 m), every three steps march one knee up and then out to the side, and then circle inward across your body, and return to the ground. Alternate legs, and repeat for the full distance.

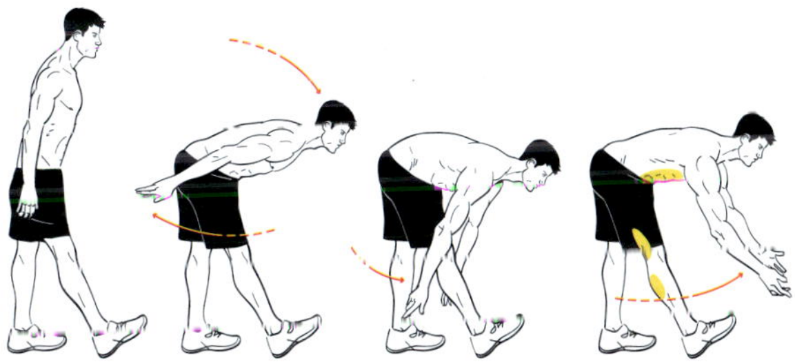

E **GROUND SWEEPS** This exercise will activate your core and stretch your calf muscles and hamstrings.

HOW Walking a distance of 20 yards (18.2 m), step forward on the right foot, swing your arms back, and then slowly sweep your arms forward, trying to brush the ground with your fingertips. Return to standing, and then repeat, leading with the left foot. Alternate legs for the full distance.

LEARN ABOUT THE LUNGE

Lunges have long been valuable components of a runner's strength-training and stretching regimen. They help you improve your coordination and balance, while working your quadriceps, hamstrings, glutes, and hip flexors. Strengthening these muscles is crucial because strong legs and hips can help protect your knees from the pounding placed on these vulnerable joints while you run. These muscles also work together to pull the body in a forward motion to increase sprinting speed, and because they are asymmetrical standing exercises (meaning you shift your body weight from one leg to the other), they challenge your balance, proprioception, and dynamic flexibility. This makes them more effective for improving your running stride compared to bilateral moves that distribute the load between both legs—such as squats, which target a similar group of muscles.

Another plus is that lunges require no equipment, and you can perform them anywhere. There are many variations, too, so you never have to get bored doing the same moves all the time. If you want to add resistance, you can perform them with resistance bands or holding a barbell, dumbbell, medicine ball, or other free weight.

A FORWARD LUNGE

WHY Targets the hips, glutes, core, and inner thighs

HOW Stand with your feet together and your hands on your hips or clasped behind your head. Lunge forward with on one leg, focusing on a downward movement of your hips until your front thigh is parallel with the floor. Firmly push off with the front leg to return to your upright, starting position. Repeat by alternating lunges with each leg leading.

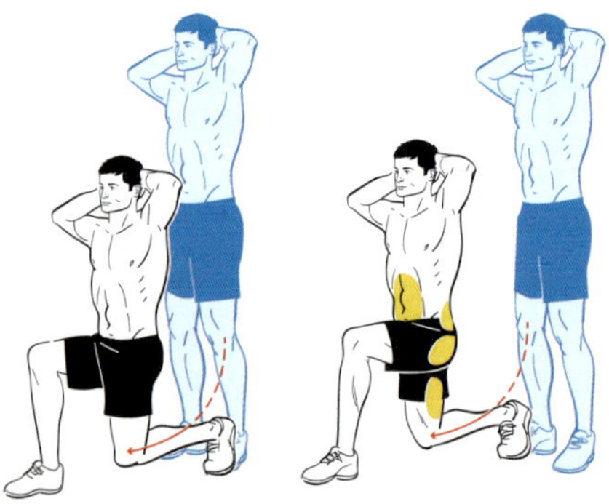

B CURTSY LUNGE

WHY Adds some torso and hip rotation while working your hips, glutes, core, and inner thighs

HOW Stand with feet together, hands on your hips or down at your sides. Take a big step back with your right leg, crossing it behind your left leg. Bend both knees and lower your body until your front thigh is parallel with the floor. Return to the starting position, and repeat on the other side.

C SKATER LUNGE

WHY Offers the usual benefits of a lunge while adding an effective cardio component

HOW Stand with your feet shoulder-width apart and your arms at your sides. Take a large step backward with your left leg, and cross it diagonally behind the right as you extend your right arm out to the side and swing the left across your hips. Hop to the left, then return to your starting position. Repeat with the other leg, and continue alternating sides.

D WALKING LUNGE

WHY Offers the benefits of a forward lunge, while it activates your core and stretches your hip flexors

HOW Stand tall with your arms at your sides. Step far forward with your right leg while simultaneously lifting up onto the ball of your left foot. With your chest high and shoulders back, bend your knees, and drop your hips downward. Press up with your right leg, and bring your left foot forward. Take another step forward, and continue alternating sides.

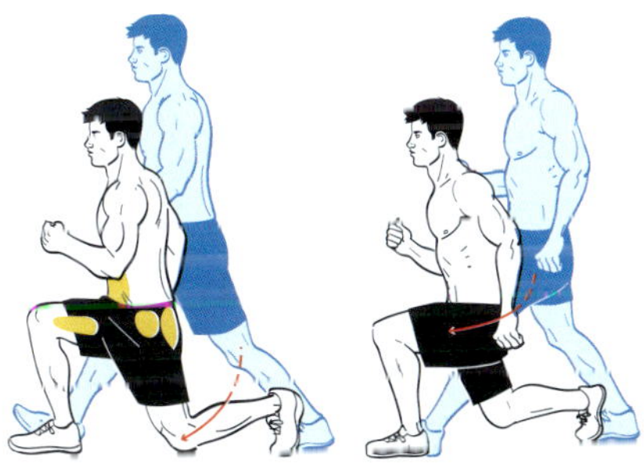

TOOLS of the TRADE

EXPLORE THE ELLIPTICAL

The elliptical trainer has become the go-to piece of equipment for those who want a thorough cardio workout that places limited stress on the joints. Also known as the cross-trainer or X-trainer, the elliptical is used to simulate stair climbing, running or walking. Simple models are self-propelled, while more deluxe models have motorized pedals with adjustable resistance and electronic consoles with readouts. The three basic types of elliptical trainers are categorized by the location of the motor, or "drive." The rear drive is the oldest design, the front-drive was a second-generation design, and the center drive incorporates the latest design technology.

To use an elliptical, adopt a comfortable standing position with your spine in a neutral position (straight back), align your knees, hips, and ankles, then distribute your weight between your heels and the balls of your feet. You then grip the handrails and move your arms with an even, controlled motion, and stride in either a forward or reverse motion, moving smoothly and continuously.

GAIN MULTIPLE BENEFITS

Depending on the speed and the resistance settings, your elliptical workout can range from light intensity to high cardio demand. Most ellipticals work the upper body (with the use of handle levers), and the lower body (via the foot pedals). Ellipticals produce an intermediate range of leg motion that is somewhere between a treadmill and a stationary bicycle, and they burn calories similar to the spin bike. In addition to offering a brisk cardio workout, the machine has other advantages.

LOW IMPACT By keeping the users' heels flat on the pedals, the machine reduces muscle and tendon stress.

FLUID MOVEMENT Users move so freely that they will experience a low relative perceived exertion (RPE), meaning they don't feel like they are working as hard as they really are.

VARIABLE STRIDES Studies have shown that the ability to vary the length of stride, a feature of late-model machines, works a larger variety of muscle groups and burns more calories—all without the user being aware of any extra work.

INEXPENSIVE HOME VERSIONS Commercial gym models might cost in the thousands of dollars, but home models can start as low as a few hundred.

TAKE IT IN INTERVALS

Interval training is one way to get the most out of your time at the gym—providing an effective cardio session that can also transform your physique. It involves alternating intense bursts of exercise with slowed-down recovery segments. You can implement it using two machines that require different rates of speed or degrees of effort or, more typically, you can work at differing levels—altering speed, incline, direction, and so on—on the same machine.

The benefits of interval training include burning more calories—even just by raising intensity for a short time—and improving aerobic capacity by increasing cardiovascular fitness, which then allows you to work longer or with more intensity. These routines alleviate the boredom of those "same old-same old" workouts, plus you can perform them on your usual equipment simply by modifying your routine.

Most up-to-date cardio machines feature a setting for interval training so you don't even have to think about configuring your session. Here are some alternative workouts on four popular machines.

ELLIPTICAL INTERVALS Adjust the workout setting to "interval," and follow the routine through periods of high and low activity with varying levels of resistance for 10 or 15 minutes. Halfway through, change the direction so you are pedalling backward.

STATIONARY BIKE INTERVALS These machines should also have an "interval" setting. Once it is set in motion, assume a "spinning" position—butt off the seat, arms braced on the handles, and your weight forward. For increased results, find a comfortable position on the seat while holding a dumbbell in each hand, and perform two sets of 10 to 12 reps of lateral raises. Or start in the same position, but this time perform two sets of 10 to 12 reps of bicep curls.

TREADMILL INTERVALS If your treadmill has an "interval" setting, activate it. Enhance your upper-body workout with punches: Hold your arms close to your body, bent at about 90 degrees, and jab outward with rotation, so that at the end of the motion your knuckles face away from your body. Alternate hands with a steady rhythm; perform for 10 to 15 minutes. Another challenging motion is the side shuffle: set the speed for two to four miles per hour, and pivot to the side, holding on to one of the handles for support, shuffling along sideways as the tread moves for 3 to 5 minutes. Or face away from the console, hold both handles, and walk or run backward.

STAIR CLIMBER INTERVALS Adjust the setting to "interval," and try one of these variations, each for 3 to 5 minutes. As you raise your left leg, swing you right leg behind you, and then alternate. Or try taking the steps two at a time. Finally, try the sidestep. Stand sideways on the machine, holding the stability bar, and carefully step up, placing one foot over the other. Midway through, pivot 180 degrees to switch directions, and lead with the opposite foot.

GYM *etiquette*

KEEP IT CLEAN

One of the reasons gym-goers carry a small towel is to dry off after a taxing workout. But don't forget to wipe down any machines or equipment you might have perspired upon. Few things in the gym experience are more distasteful than sliding onto damp seats or gripping sweaty handles—left by the previous user. Some people even carry two towels—one for personal hygiene and one to swipe over equipment before and after they use it.

WALK THIS WAY

It might surprise you to know that walking at a brisk pace burns roughly two-thirds of the calories that outright running does—113 calories per mile walked versus 151 per mile run. Once those large muscles in your limbs and core get set in motion calories get incinerated. So don't feel you have to hit the treadmill at the highest setting or pound the pavement to get a good cardio workout. Walking is a low-impact activity, which makes it ideal for seniors or those with joint issues, plus it can be a great gateway activity to running.

Trainers recommend mixing up your walking workout to avoid getting into a rut. Push yourself on the treadmill by trying programs that vary the speed and incline, and add in days on the elliptical or stair climber—or take it outdoors every do often if the weather permits.

Walking—or power walking, which also includes exaggerated arm swinging—helps you maintain a proper weight and prevent or manage heart disease, high blood pressure, and type 2 diabetes. It strengthens bones and muscles and even improves your mood. Even on days when you can't make it to the gym you can get in some steps—you don't need extra equipment or special clothing, and it's something you likely do every day already. You simply need to increase your volume of steps and build your intensity to aerobic levels.

TWEAK YOUR TECHNIQUE

"Tweak what?" you think. "It's only walking!" But the truth is, just as with any form of exercise, to benefit most, you need to perform it properly. As you walk, aim for good posture, an easy stride, a tight core, and purposeful movements.

WARM UP Always walk slowly for the first 5 or 10 minutes.

LOOK AHEAD Keep your head up, so that you are gazing forward, not at the ground.

GO EASY Relax your neck, shoulders, and back, so that you are not standing stiffly upright.

STAY LOOSE As you walk, swing your arms freely, with a slight bend in the elbows. A little arm pumping is also okay.

TIGHTEN UP As you move forward, tighten your stomach muscles, and make sure your back is straight, not arched forward or backward.

SMOOTH OUT Make sure you are walking with a smooth gait, rolling your foot from heel to toe.

COOL DOWN Every brisk walk needs a period of cooling down—try five minutes of slow walking followed, perhaps, by some dynamic muscle stretches.

CHOOSE YOUR SHOES

For walking on a track, sidewalk, or street, shoes need to have proper arch support; firm, thick heels; and thick, flexible soles to cushion your feet and act as shock absorbers. Some makers of athletic gear offer walking shoes with more techie features—orthotic footbed inserts, gel pads in the heels, or reflective panels for walking at night.

If hiking is your thing, it's critical to invest in good quality footwear. Hiking shoes, usually worn for day hikes, are low-cut with flexible midsoles. Mid- or high-cut flexible hiking boots are used for both day hikes and weekend backpacking. High-cut backpacking boots are the sturdy, supportive option, designed for carrying heavy loads through back country on trips of multiple days.

HIKE FOR HEALTH

Hiking—walking outdoors across varied terrain, especially woodlands or hills—can supply a great cardio-respiratory session. Hiking works nearly every part of the body: legs, knees, ankles, arms, hips, glutes, abs, shoulders, and neck. And like any weight-bearing activity, it lowers your risk of heart disease, improves blood sugar and blood pressure levels, and boosts bone density. A person weighing 155 pounds (70 kg) burns an average of 370 calories for every hour of hiking. And you needn't be in tip-top shape to begin—start with easy routes through relatively level areas, and work your way up to steeper, more demanding terrain.

You can map new treks and share your favorite routes with other hikers online or on your phone with apps such as MapMyHike. To get detailed terrain maps, try offline GPS apps like BackCountry Navigator or MotionX GPS.

And while of course the whole point of hiking is to get out in the great outdoors, you can greatly benefit by using your gym time to improve your hiking experience. Step classes or time on the elliptical build endurance, while squats, lunges, and core exercises make it easier to scramble up steep trails. Speak to a personal trainer about building a resistance program geared to your outdoor-fitness plans and goals.

BRING THE FAM

Hiking can be a great family wellness activity. Children get many of the same benefits as adults, as well as lowering their risk factors for heart disease, high blood pressure, type 2 diabetes, depression, and sleep disorders. Decreased levels of stress can make children more ready to learn in school. And just think of the good example you're setting—for many kids who are encouraged to be active during their formative years, fitness becomes a lifelong habit.

TOOLS of the TRADE

RIDE A STATIONARY BIKE

Also known as the exercise bike or exercycle, the stationary bicycle is a special-purpose exercise machine with a saddle, pedals, and handlebars—but no actual wheels—that offers outstanding cardio benefits. The pedals provide adjustable resistance to increase the intensity of the exercise; some models even allow the user to pedal backward to work the antagonist muscles. These bikes typically have a crankshaft and bottom bracket that powers a flywheel by means of a belt or chain. Specialized models that use weighted flywheels at the front are known as spinners. While spinners and stationary bikes imitate the form of a regular bike, recumbent bikes provide back support with low, chairlike seats.

Stationary bicycles are not only great for improving cardio fitness and achieving weight loss, they are also a long-valued tool of physical therapists, primarily because of the safe, low-impact, and effective workouts they provide. Exercise bikes are even used on the International Space Station; called veloergometers, they counter the cardiovascular de-conditioning that can occur in a microgravity environment.

Ask the EXPERT

WHICH BIKE POSITION IS BEST?

Your goal when performing stationary bike cardio is to accelerate your metabolism, and there is little difference between cycling upright and pedaling in the recumbent position. A recumbent bike does, however, allow you to rest your lower-back muscles, while cycling without this feature forces you to use your core muscles to support your torso. For those with back pain, the recumbent style is probably the better choice—upright models can put too much stress on vulnerable lower-back muscles.

TRY A CYCLING CLASS

Gold's Gym, along with many others, offer intense cycle classes, where members on stationary bikes follow an instructor—often with the added bonus of lively music and lighting effects. These classes typically focus on metabolic intervals—from light to heavy resistance that challenges but rarely fatigue the muscles—making them ideal for most age groups. Cycle classes burn calories, improve cardiovascular health, offer an effective yet low-impact workout, and help you achieve tighter abs and toned, attractive legs. And if you can't always keep up, simply progress at your own pace. Cycling aficionados say they often leave class with high energy and a feeling of euphoria.

STAY HEALTHY

GYM *etiquette*

On any given day in the average gym, dozens of people will end up using a particular piece of equipment, whether it's a barbell or dumbbells, squat rack or bench press, treadmill or stationary bike—and a lot of those people are going to work up a sweat. With this in mind, bring a small hand towel with you and be sure to wipe down the area you've used. It's not only polite, but it also helps prevent the spread of colds or other communicable illnesses. Once again, courtesy and consideration are primary in the close confines of the gym floor.

HIT HIGH INTENSITY ON THE STATIONARY BIKE

The experts at Gold's Gym developed these four high-intensity interval (HIIT) workouts for the stationary bike. To perform this regimen, first determine your MHR, or maximum heart rate, and then add a new HIIT set to your cardio routine each week for four weeks, but avoid doing them on consecutive days.

WEEK 1: 30-MINUTE WORKOUTS

WORKOUT 1

- 10-minute warm-up at 65 percent MHR
- 30-second sprint at 75 percent MHR, then 60 seconds recovery at 65 percent MHR
- Repeat for 15 minutes
- 5-minute cool-down at 65 percent MHR

WORKOUT 2

- 10-minute warm-up at 65 percent MHR
- 30-second sprint at 75 percent MHR, then 90 seconds recovery at 65 percent MHR
- Repeat the above intervals for 15 minutes
- 5-minute cool-down at 65 percent MHR

WEEK 2: 35-MINUTE WORKOUTS

WORKOUT 1

- 10-minute warm-up at 65 percent MHR
- 30-second sprint at 80 percent MHR, then 60 seconds recovery at 65 percent MHR
- Repeat for 15 minutes
- 10-minute cool-down at 65 percent MHR

WORKOUT 2

- 10-minute warm-up at 65 percent MHR
- 30-second sprint at 80 percent MHR, then 90 seconds recovery at 65 percent MHR
- Repeat the above intervals for 15 minutes
- 10-minute cool-down at 65 percent MHR

WEEK 3: 40-MINUTE WORKOUTS

WORKOUT 1

- 10-minute warm-up at 65 percent MHR
- 30-second sprint at 85 percent MHR, then 60 seconds recovery at 65 percent MHR
- Repeat for 15 minutes
- 15-minute cool-down at 65 percent MHR

WORKOUT 2

- 10-minute warm-up at 65 percent MHR
- 30-second sprint at 85 percent MHR, then 90 seconds recovery at 65 percent MHR
- Repeat for 15 minutes
- 15-minute cool-down at 65 percent MHR

WEEK 4: 45-MINUTE WORKOUTS

WORKOUT 1

- 10-minute warm-up at 65 percent MHR
- 45-second sprint at 85 percent MHR, then 90 seconds recovery at 65 percent MHR
- Repeat for 15 minutes
- 20-minute cool-down at 65 percent MHR

WORKOUT 2

- 10-minute warm-up at 65 percent MHR
- 45-second sprint at 85 percent MHR, then 120 seconds recovery at 65 percent MHR
- Repeat for 15 minutes
- 20-minute cool-down at 65 percent MHR

FREEWHEEL FOR FITNESS

Riding a traditional bicycle outdoors offers the same health benefits as using a stationary bike in the gym: a great cardio workout, effective body toning, increased weight loss, and low-impact exercise, but has the additional pluses of diverse scenery, variable terrain, and changing elevations. And then there is the longevity factor—many bike enthusiasts are able to keep riding well into their golden years.

A bicycle is also legitimate transportation. Try using your bike to commute to work, visit friends, head over to the library, or to do some shopping. Once you make bike-riding a regular part of your life, you will anticipate that rush of exhilaration whenever you pedal out into the street—a throwback, perhaps, to your childhood, when hopping onto a bicycle meant complete freedom.

If you want to track your biking action, try apps like Cyclemeter and Strava.

CHOOSE THE RIGHT WHEELS

There are currently a number of bicycle styles on the market. Before you decide on a model, ask yourself these questions: Where do you intend to ride, and will you ride for pleasure or for utility? Who do you normally ride with, and what sort of bikes do they use? (You'll want a bike that can keep up.) What was it that you like or dislike about previous bikes you've owned? To help you make the right choice, the following chart lists the most popular bike models and covers their features and uses.

TYPE	FEATURES	USAGE
ROAD BIKE	Lightweight frame; skinny tires; drop handlebars; multiple gears	Made to be ridden fast on smooth pavement; also called a "racer"
TOURING BIKE	More sturdy than a road bike; drop handlebars; low gear range	Made for distance riding; rider sits more up right than on a road bike; good for commuting
MOUNTAIN BIKE	Shock absorbers; rugged tires; flat or upright handlebars; very low gear range	Meant for off-road terrain and unpaved trails
HYBRID BIKE	Large padded seat; upright handlebars; medium tires with semi-smooth tread	Offers advantages of both a road and mountain bike; meant for casual riding around town or on bike paths
CRUISER BIKE	Large, comfortable seat; wide balloon tires; upright/swept-back handlebars; single speed/three speed; coaster brake	Made for casual riding and running errands in a high, upright position

CRUISE IN COMFORT

Clothing for serious cyclists is form fitting and aerodynamic, typically made of fabrics that wick away moisture and keep you cool. Tops and shorts are also available in compression fabrics. Bike jerseys come in many patterns and colors—opt for the brighter ones that make you more visible to automobile and truck drivers. In winter, try a cold-weather jersey or a cycling jacket that allows your body to air out.

If you are planning a long ride or just intend to ride often, invest in bicycle shorts that feature a padded seat your butt will thank you. For colder weather, try donning cycling tights over your shorts. You should also consider purchasing fingerless riding gloves, biking shoes that allow you to clip your feet into the bike pedals, and biking socks that wick moisture away and keep your feet aired out. Face masks made from compression material that keep your face warm and protected from the elements are another cold-weather option.

Always check the weather report before a ride to make sure you dress appropriately. And after your ride, wash your clothes immediately to prevent the growth of bacteria.

PROTECT YOUR HEAD

Always wear a helmet when cycling, even if you are just "going down the street." A minor fall could still cause serious brain injury. And don't cheap out at a discount store—buy a quality helmet from a reputable bike shop. If it's cold outside, you can use a helmet cover or wear an approved head covering under it—or both (it's dangerous to just add a beanie or bandana, as this may change the helmet's fit).

FUEL UP AND PEDAL

Make sure to eat breakfast before a morning ride—even if it's just instant oatmeal or a fruit smoothie—to replenish your liver's glycogen stores. During long rides, refuelling can be tricky; try filling your water bottle with a sports beverage, or stash healthy snacks in your jersey. Also make sure to eat some "recovery food," say, a sandwich and a salad, within 30 to 60 minutes of ending your ride. Needless to say, staying hydrated throughout your ride is key—take a sip at least every 15 minutes—then refill your bottle at ride's end, and drink it within an hour.

TAKE YOUR BIKE TO WORK

Many studies have shown that exercise relieves stress, and so it's not surprising that those who commute to their jobs via bicycle report lower stress levels than those who use cars ... and sit stewing in rush-hour traffic or those who are at the mercy of mass transit. Studies have found that a much higher rate of biking commuters reported enjoying their commute than those who took alternate forms of transportation to work.

TARGETED workout

POWER YOUR PEDALING

Every year, Gold's Gym teams up with the American Diabetes Association to sponsor Tour de Cure, a series of fund-raising cycling events held nationwide. If you participate in this kind of event, hours in the saddle can fatigue your abs and lower back, making it difficult for your to maintain strong cycling form.

Below are exercises that will help keep your core stabilized and solid. Cycling is a non-weight-bearing activity, so it's smart to also strength train your lower body. The more strength you build in your glutes, quads, and hamstrings, the easier it will be to power up hills and maintain an efficient pedal stroke.

Whether you plan to take part in a competitive cycling event or just want to be in shape for rides around town, incorporate the following exercises into your training program to improve your cycling efficiency and decrease your risk of injury.

For each exercise, aim for three sets of 20 reps each, with a 60-second rest between sets.

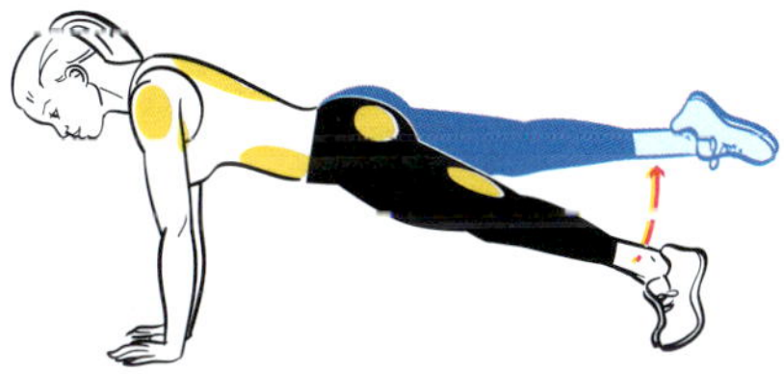

A **PLANK WITH GLUTE RAISE** Combining the classic core-strengthening plank with a glute raise will target your abs, pecs, delts, back, glutes, and hamstrings.

HOW Get into plank position with arms extended as if you were about to do a push-up. (Too hard? Modify it by supporting your weight on your forearms.) With your glutes, lift your right leg off the floor until it's in line with your back, then pause. Lower, and keep alternating legs.

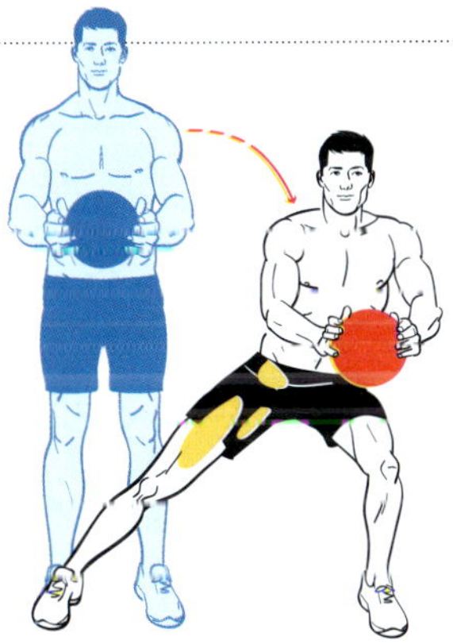

B **SIDE LUNGE** This lunge adds emphasis to your hip adductors as it works your quads.

HOW Start with your feet together and your arms at your sides. Step sideways into a long lunge, keeping your planted leg straight. Bend your knee to form a 90-degree angle. Press back up with your bended leg, and return to the starting position. For an advanced version, hold a medicine ball.

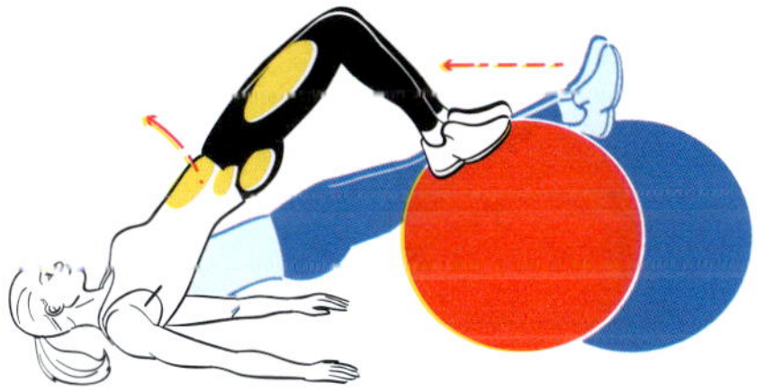

C **STABILITY BALL BRIDGE** A bridge is another classic core stabilizer—and adding the stability ball amps up the stabilizing effect to work your abs, hips, quads, and glutes.

HOW Lie flat on the floor with your heels resting on a stability ball. Lift your hips off the floor as you pull the ball toward your butt with your feet. Roll the ball away from you, and lower your hips.

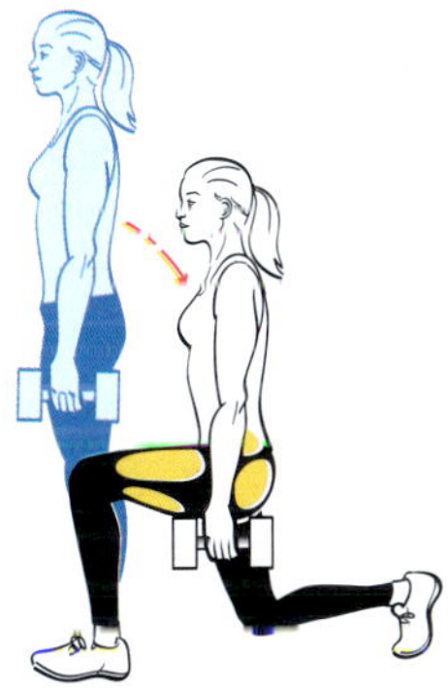

D **REVERSE LUNGE** A reverse lunge will give you a thorough lower-body workout, targeting your hamstrings, quads, glutes, and hips.

HOW Start with feet shoulder-width apart. Lunge behind youwith your right leg as if you were about to take a big step backward. Pause there for a moment, before returning to the starting position. Repeat with your left leg. For an advanced version, hold a pair of dumbbells at your sides.

GET PHYSICAL

The allure of the aerobics class, popularized by the press and Hollywood in the 1980s (especially those iconic Jane Fonda exercise videos), has never faded. This kind of fitness class, which features rhythmic strength and stretching moves performed to music, gives you high cardio value and can be a whole lot of fun. Instructors lead class members in routines composed of dancelike exercises that are geared to different levels of intensity and complexity. Most gyms offer a range of aerobics options designed for specific levels of experience, including seniors. A well-balanced class typically consists of 5 to 10 minutes of warming up, followed by 25 to 30 for cardio conditioning, 10 to 15 minutes of strength conditioning, followed by 5 to 8 minutes of cooling down, and then finally, 5 to 8 more for stretching and flexibility moves.

STEP IT UP!

Step aerobics adds an elevated platform, which you mount and dismount in tempo. Some platforms feature adjustable heights for varying levels of intensity. The basic 4-beat step calls for you to place one foot on the platform, followed by the other, and then removing them in the same order. Variations include the corner kick, repeater knee, T-step, lunge, straddle down, and many more. The class instructor combines these moves, typically timing them to 32 beats per set. More advanced choreography may include turns, mambos, and stomps. Class members learn the various steps during class and then perform two or three complete routines at the end.

Steps aerobics classes can help you burn fat and calories, reduce stress, foster good sleep habits, strengthen muscles, and create a sleek, streamlined physique. As with regular aerobics classes—or most any class—you can proceed at a comfortable pace until you feel strong enough to complete the entire routine.

BE A CLASS ACT

Taking classes is a great way to tone up and have fun. Classes are perfect for beginners and those returning to the gym: you'll find motivation, accountability, and structure in a group that solo workouts lack. But with so many choices, which classes are right for you? Gold's Gym recommends first determining which fitness issues you want to tackle. To improve overall well-being, cardio classes—including fast-paced interval training—are the best way to go. Gold's Gym's BODYATTACK classes are high-energy interval training, sports-inspired cardio workouts for building strength and stamina. To give your physique a long, lean look with excellent flexibility, try yoga or Pilates classes, or try a dance-based class like BODYJAM. To burn calories, increase endurance, and build leg strength, take a cycling class. For a powerful full-body workout that lets you "unleash the beast," mixed martial arts could be the answer.

Once you decide to sample a class or two, you might need some guidance on how to get the most out of the experience. Here are some of the insights from the fitness experts at Gold's Gym for doing just that in any exercise class.

ARRIVE PREPARED Get to class early, bring a towel and a water bottle, and wear supportive sneakers and comfortable clothing that allows you to move easily. If you're new, introduce yourself to the instructor, and mention any injuries or medical conditions that could affect how you exercise.

FIND YOUR SPOT Try to position yourself near the front of the class with a good view of the instructor. If you have questions, ask them after class.

SEEK YOUR LEVEL During class, the instructor may show you how to modify an exercise to make it easier or more challenging. Do the version that you're more comfortable with.

TAKE A BREAK Some classes, like weight lifting, should not be taken two days in a row. Allow a cardio day or rest day in between—and try to add some yoga or stretching to the mix.

RESERVE JUDGMENT Attend at least three sessions of a new class before you decide whether or not it's for you. By the third session, you'll be familiar with the movements and exercises and can make an informed decision.

STAY FOR STRETCHING Don't bolt as soon as the heart-thumping action ends. Remember, you will burn more calories post workout if you allow yourself time to stretch.

LET THE MUSIC DRIVE YOU

As anyone who dances for a living can tell you, dancing takes a lot of hard work. Yet the many benefits of this activity make it worth all the effort—dancing offers a total-body workout that conditions the heart and lungs, strengthens your muscles and skeletal system, reduces bone loss, increases flexibility and joint mobility, and improves coordination and balance. There is also evidence that dancing can heighten your brainpower and improve your mental outlook. In research studies that compared dancers to non-dancers, there was evidence that dancing preserves both perceptual abilities and motor skills. What's not to love?

The rhythmic response we have to the beat of throbbing music is hard-wired into our brains. Musical vibrations actually light up timing circuits within our brains that prompt us to start moving in tempo. These same circuits are entwined with our communication and memory systems—which is why certain songs can evoke such a strong emotional response. This is also why working out to music can feel so fulfilling: it satisfies us on several levels. And the more time we spend dancing, the more our brains learn to release those pleasurable feelings, eventually leaving us with a more positive outlook and a strong sense of well-being.

SIGN UP FOR A DANCE CLASS

For years, fans of dance who wanted to learn ballet, jazz, tap, Latin, or ballroom dance had to go to specialized studios and pay for expensive classes—and rarely got a real cardio workout. Within the last few decades, gyms have begun offering "dancercise" classes that incorporate dance moves into fitness routines. Today, many gyms allow you to choose from a number of traditional dance classes—salsa, ballet or barre work, and swing. Or, if you're feeling particularly adventurous, you can find a workout based on pole dancing, jazz moves, or even acrobatics, to let your inner circus performer come out to play.

Gold's Gym offers a number of dance-inspired cardio classes that take inspiration from jazz, ballet, salsa, hip hop and other sources to create cardio routines that are fun and easy to follow. If you want to dance in your living room, you can also try Gold's Gym Dance Workout for the Nintendo Wii game system.

DANCE

GET YOUR GROOVE ON

In addition to traditional dance classes, a new generation of dance-exercise has arisen, which incorporates choreographed dance moves with fitness routines and a fun atmosphere that feels more like a dance party than a traditional cardio class—while still burning hundreds of calories an hour.

Classes feature dance-based exercises to get your heart pumping and your body moving to the beat while often also incorporating some bodyweight-based resistance work for a full-body workout. If you're recovering from an injury, or just enjoy a different set of challenges, look for dance-based "aquarobics" classes that take place in a pool.

Whether you're trying out a class based on world music, old-school disco, or the latest club moves, be assured that you'll have fun whether or not you have any dance experience.

Popular classes are often crowded and heat up, so wear layers of clothing you can shed, and wear supportive shoes that allow you to easily pivot. And don't forget your heart-rate monitor to keep track of how hard you're working.

THINK *about it*

In a recent study, cardiac patients who danced three times a week for 20 minutes saw their heart health improve significantly more than patients who stuck to traditional cardio routines.

TUNE IN AND TONE

In conjunction with the annual March Music Madness contest, when gym members vote on their favorite workout tunes in a bracket-style competition, Gold's Gym has come up with four dance moves guaranteed to work your groove thing.

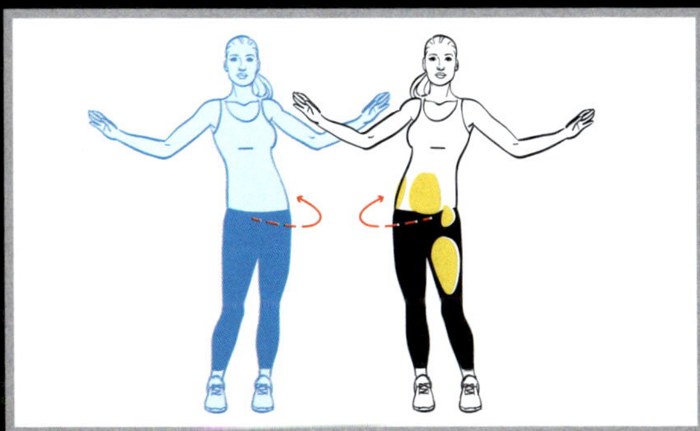

A **BELLY DANCE** This undulating Middle Eastern move works the abs, hips, and thighs. Repeat for two counts of eight.

HOW Stand with your feet hip-width apart, your knees slightly bent, and your arms extended to the sides. Create a figure 8 with your hips, swaying to the left front, side, and back,, and then sway to the right front, side, and back.

B **THE TWIST** Chubby Checker's dance sensation is still a great way to sculpt abs, thighs, and glutes. Perform one count of eight standing, and then lower to the floor twisting for one count of eight.

HOW Begin with your feet shoulder-width apart and your arms extended out to the sides. Stand on the balls of your feet, and rotate your hips, torso, and legs as a single unit while keeping your arms stationary. As you twist, lower yourself with knees bent and back straight until the backs of your quads hit your calves. Repeat, alternating directions.

C **KNEE KICKS** These lively chorus line moves shape your legs, abs, and shoulders. Repeat with each leg four times.

HOW Stand tall, with your feet together and your arms out to the sides. Hop on both feet, and then lift your left leg with your knee bent to 90 degrees. Hop on both feet again, and then raise your right leg. You can also kick with a straight leg on each side, or alternate bent leg and straight leg.

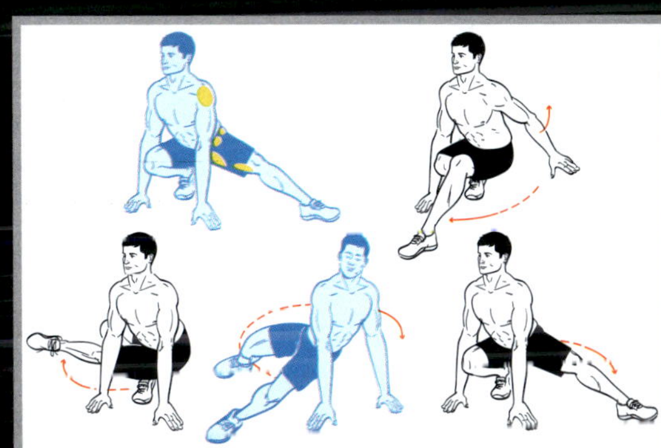

D **PINWHEEL** This old-school break dance move tones the upper body and works the core. Do eight sets on each side.

HOW Lower into a squat, with the back of your thighs touching your calves. Place both hands on the floor in front of you, and extend your left leg straight to the side. Move your left leg in a forward circle all the way around your body, lifting first your left arm, then the right arm, then the right foot (hopping over the leg.)

PRACTICE MARTIAL ARTS

Although hand-to-hand martial arts, such as wrestling and grappling—which simulated combat situations—were practiced for millennia, in the late 19th century Asian-style martial arts began to spread beyond their national borders. Adults and youngsters in many parts of the globe eventually embraced disciplines such as jiu jitsu and judo from Japan, kung fu from China, and taekwondo from Korea. The TV series *Kung Fu* and the movie *The Karate Kid,* plus a host of Asian martial arts films, helped broaden the appeal during the 1960s and '70s. Soon dojos (training facilities—the Japanese term actually translates as "place of the way") began to crop up in many cities. The practice of these martial arts disciplines not only provides a useful fitness tool for adults, many behaviorists discovered that they help children release much of their pent-up energy.

Today, people of all ages pursue a range of martial arts. Enlightened martial artists like to point out that the study of any style will ultimately benefit the student. Some of the most popular options are listed below.

AIKIDO Practitioners of this Japanese grappling art learn to flow with the motion of the attacker.

JUDO The goal of this relatively modern Japanese defensive art is to throw the opponent to the ground or grapple with them until they are immobile. Judo and taekwondo are the only Asian martial arts sanctioned by the Olympic Games.

JIU JITSU This Japanese discipline is aimed at defeating an armed or armored opponent with no weapon or only a short weapon. The Brazilian version, with its throws, takedowns, and sweeps, provides a good method of self-defense for women.

KARATE Developed in Okinawa, Japan, karate stresses striking techniques such as punching, kicking, knee and elbow strikes, and open-hand techniques.

KRAV MAGA Developed in Israel, this form of hand-to-hand combat, which combines wrestling, grappling, and striking techniques, is known for its lack of rules and its variety of brutal counterattacks.

KUNG FU OR WUSHU These are the umbrella terms for the hundreds of defensive arts of China. There are scores of styles or schools, and some mimic animal movements, such as Eagle Claw, Five Animals (Shaolin), Monkey, Praying Mantis, and Wing Chun. The Shaolin form of kung fu is regarded as one of the first codified styles of Chinese martial arts.

MUAY THAI (THAI BOXING) This tough Thailand discipline uses stand-up striking and clinching techniques incorporating punching, kicking, and knee and elbow strikes—involving eight points of contact—as well as fight strategies.

TAEKWONDO The popular Korean art of self-defense dates back by more than 2,000 years. It utilizes punches, blocks, takedowns, throws, and open-hand strikes, and it emphasizes high kicks requiring explosive action, speed, and agility.

WRESTLING While wrestling offers a great cardio workout, it also features dangerous takedowns and body manipulations, and so is not for the injury prone.

MIX IT UP WITH MMA

Mixed martial arts (MMA) is a full-contact sport that combines several martial- and nonmartial-arts disciplines that, over time, have morphed into one cohesive style. This is a demanding pursuit, requiring familiarity with many skills and positions, as well as speed, endurance, strength, and agility. Practitioners typically have to master Brazilian jiu jitsu, wrestling, muay Thai, and aspects of taekwondo. As a result, MMA athletes are among the fittest in the world. Most gyms support the study of MMA without the actual fighting matches, although light sparring is allowed. Many Gold's Gyms offer classes in MMA—check their website for a gym near you, and click on the class schedule to check for days and times.

TRY OUT KICKBOXING

Karate, a striking art incorporating punching, kicking, knee and elbow strikes, and karate-chop "knife hands," is one of the most popular martial arts. Karate became widely known in North America after World War II servicemen studied it in Asia and opened karate schools back home.

In the 1960s, a new discipline arose in Japan, dubbed kickboxing. This concept encompassed stand-up combat sports that incorporate both kicking and punching, and developed from karate as well as Muay Thai and Western boxing. At first, kickboxing was practiced as a form of self-defense and a competitive sport, then as a fitness regimen. In the 1990s, a more aerobics-friendly version was developed called Tae Bo.

As a fitness tool, kickboxing with a heavy bag provides a terrific workout that increases heart rate, burns fat, and builds muscle. Punches employed include the jab, cross, hook, and uppercut, and kicks include the front, side, and roundhouse. The average person will expend 800 to 1,200 calories per class. No wonder trainers warn newbies that they are likely to feel exhausted after their first few workouts, and, meanwhile, their metabolism will hum along 10 to 15 percent higher than normal for the next 18 hours.

Gold's Gym offers kickboxing classes in some locations; check their website for days and times. Here are some tips for starting out (and don't forget to bring a towel).

GATHER YOUR GEAR Wear loose workout clothing and shoes that allow you to move from side to side.

WARM UP Before approaching the weight bag, perform a few minutes of light calisthenics, some stretching, and body-weight exercises.

ADOPT A FIGHTING STANCE Before you land a punch, practice the basic stance in the mirror until you get it right. Start with feet shoulder-width apart, knees slightly bent. Hold your right hand up near your ear, and keep your left hand in front of your face with elbows down, near your body.

LEARN TO PUNCH A jab is quick surprise punch aimed at an imaginary nose. A cross is a straight punch thrown from the rear hand. A hook is a circular punch from the lead hand, with a cheek or ear being the imaginary target. An uppercut is a thrusting punch to the chin delivered from the rear hand, fist pointing at the ceiling.

KICK UP YOUR HEELS The basic front kick is delivered with the heel—imagine kicking a door closed using your raised foot. The roundhouse kick is circular, with your leg moving in an arc, as if you were slapping the target with your shoelaces. The intimidating side kick is powered by the glutes; think of it as kicking through a target with your heel.

DE-STRESS WITH TAI CHI

T'ai chi ch'uan is one of more than 300 Chinese martial arts. There are many forms of tai chi, both traditional and modern, but the five most practiced, Yang, Chen, Wu, Sun, and Woo, were derived from the original Chen family style. Initially tai chi was performed as defensive training, with an emphasis on strength, speed, flexibility, and balance in Mandarin, the name literally translates as "supreme ultimate boxing." Over time, it evolved into a slow, soft, gentle form of exercise, with flowing motions, that can be practiced by those of all ages. Advocates call it the "ultimate low-impact workout."

Tai chi's health benefits include the ability to elevate heart rate, ease stress levels, lower blood pressure, improve balance, posture, and circulation, and even increase longevity. According to gait and balance experts, tai chi offers the best biomechanical scenarios for keeping a person stable. Perhaps the nicest benefit, users (even seniors) tend to leave their sessions feeling empowered.

Some Gold's Gym locations offer classes in tai chi; check their website for places and dates.

PUNCH IT OUT

Boxing—it's not just for pugilists anymore. Nope, not since gymgoers of all kinds discovered that learning basic boxing moves in a class or taking repeated shots at the heavy bag is a great way to tone up, increase cardiovascular fitness and coordination, and build muscle—not to mention that they also get to work off a ton of aggression and stress.

The sport of boxing, which is roughly 80 percent anaerobic and 20 percent aerobic, targets the entire body and furnishes what might just be the ultimate HIIT workout. It is a demanding pursuit that requires strong endurance, hand-eye coordination, power, and a certain amount of nerve—even if you don't ever actually climb into a ring. Here are some basic tips to follow to make sure you are "fighting in the proper weight class."

GET TONED The toning effects of boxing comes from the way in which you punch—your lower-back and abdominal muscles provide power by initiating an explosive hip turn, while your arms and shoulders bear the brunt of the muscle recruitment that's needed to strike hard and fast. A consistent boxing regimen can add significant definition to these areas and even create mass.

TAKE A CLASS If the thought of boxing intimidates you, try learning the basic moves—punches, footwork, and defensive maneuvers—in a class with a qualified instructor. And don't be afraid: there is no contact between you and other participants in the class: these sessions are meant to hone your technique, but they can also be a great body workout and a ton of fun.

FIND A TRAINER Even if you aren't scheduling any Golden Gloves matches, consider visiting a boxing gym and booking a few hours with a real trainer, someone who can teach you how to strike properly. Boxing can be a jarring, contact-heavy activity, and you shouldn't just find a heavy bag and start whaling on it. A good coach can help you develop the right technique, teach you to pace yourself, cut down your risk of injury, and help keep you from developing bad habits.

DO YOUR RESEARCH If you can't hire a pro trainer, research technique as much as you can. Remember that the average human body is not geared to repeatedly generate these types of forces. Furthermore, maintaining the proper technique allows you to benefit from a sport that provides multiple levels of fitness.

DANCE AND JAB Begin by dancing around the bag and applying the basic punches—the hook, the cross, and the uppercut—and incorporating the jab. After three rounds or so, spend one round just using the jab, making sure to perfect your strike. (This is the most important punch in boxing because it sets up everything else you do.)

SWITCH SIDES After your jab-only round, try switching hands. If you are right-handed, now lead with your left. This is beneficial to your body and your central nervous system, and teaches you how to deploy your jab and power punches with both hands.

PICK UP THE PACE Once you have mastered the rhythm you need to complete your individual rounds, increase the intensity during the last 30 seconds of each round. Stay in place instead of dancing, and use punishing power punches on the bag.

THINK INSIDE THE BOXING RING

Suppose you decide you actually want to engage in some sparring with a partner to experience the thrill of taking a punch and returning one. How would you go about arranging it? The good news is that some gyms—including the Gold's Gym facility in Los Angeles, California—feature a boxing ring. Another alternative is to contact a boxing gym, and ask if they know of other amateur boxers who are looking to spar. (There are two types of boxing gyms, those that cater to boxers-in-training and those that offer boxing to other athletes as a way to get in shape. You want the former, although some gyms do both.) Obviously, you don't want to get into the ring with a prizefighter, but there are bound to be other boxers at your level who are also looking for ring experience. Or contact a pro trainer, if you used one, and ask him to check around for potential partners.

There are also new boxing franchises opening up that are moving away from the gritty, sweaty, old-school boxing facilities of the *Rocky* films and creating fresh athletic environments that are welcoming to almost everyone.

BOX YOUR SHADOW

Shadow boxing enables you to practice the boxing techniques that you've learned, as well as allow you to try out various combinations of punches. You simply box in front of a mirror, imagining your reflection as your opponent. It's great as a warm-up or a way to fill your time if the heavy bag is in use. It also let you check your stance and footwork and to make sure you are properly keeping your guard up.

BECOME BOXER FIT

Boxing itself is a type of exercise, but it is a taxing and demanding one, so it may make sense to train yourself up to it with other forms of exercise. Consider a combination of upper-body resistance work and skipping, running, jumping rope, calisthenics, and wind sprints.

TAKE THE PLUNGE

Like biking and rowing, swimming is an athletic discipline that gives the whole body a workout, benefiting the cardiovascular and respiratory system, the core, arms, shoulders, legs, glutes, and back. And because humans are buoyant in water, aquatic workouts—whether done swimming or standing—tend to be low impact, even gentle on the body. This makes swimming ideal for exercising when recovering from injury. On the other hand, the weight of water offers resistance as you move through it, creating an opportunity for building strength. Another plus is that even though you are raising your heart rate, the water keeps your body cool, so you can perform longer than, say, running on a hot, humid day. Fans of swimming also point out that it is fun and relaxing.

If you make swimming part of your fitness regimen, plan on spending two and half hours in the water each week. Warm up with some light cardio and stretches, then start with a low- to medium-intensity workout of laps. Gradually build up the impact by swimming faster or by doing more laps. Ideally, you want to swim in a pool, where you can monitor your mileage, but if you go for a swim in the ocean or a lake, plot the distance between two landmarks on shore, and swim between them. In open water, never swim alone, and make sure you know how to stay safe when dealing with currents.

LEARN BASIC SWIM STROKES

If you crave the benefits of swimming, but don't know how or never mastered a proper stroke beyond a dog paddle, you can take classes at community pools and many gyms. It's important to know how to swim, if only for the sake of your safety, even if you never use it for exercise.

There are a number of different competitive strokes—which most of us see during the summer Olympics—but the most common ones for recreational swimming are the speedy freestyle (or front crawl), the fluid backstroke, and the calm, relaxed breaststroke.

STROKE	DESCRIPTION	BENEFITS
FREESTYLE	Arms alternately stroke with a windmill motion; face is down in the water, head turns to one side to breathe as that arm rises; knees together; legs kick powerfully	As you gain speed, laps fly by; works the chest muscles, the lats, and other back muscles.
BACKSTROKE	Start by floating on your back with hands at your sides. Your arms alternately stroke up and back over your head as you simultaneously flutter kick your legs.	Great for recovery swims between intense workouts; engages the lats and hamstrings.
BREASTSTROKE	Feet together; bend knees, bring feet up to butt, then kick out to sides with froglike whip kick; at same time, arms push forward from chest, separate, move in a circular stroke, return to chest.	Perform with face in or out of water; easy on the body, therefore good for beginners.

SYNCHRONIZE YOUR MOVES

Water aerobics classes, or aqua fitness, offer the benefit of low-impact exercise while getting your heart pumping and your body moving. Because they are easy on the joints, these classes are favorites of seniors, but they are great for anyone who wants to increase fitness levels. Classes may include work with buoyant hand weights or noodles, dancing, or Zumba. Some of the basic moves are listed below.

JOG IN PLACE Show great energy; keep your knees high.

TICK-TOCK HOP Quickly jump from side to side with your feet together.

KNEE TWIST Cross your right elbow toward your left knee at your waist. Alternate sides.

SQUAT JUMP Squat down with arms extended at shoulder height; jump as high as possible while raising arms overhead.

OUTER-THIGH LIFT Stand with left side at wall, feet together, holding edge with left hand. Lift right leg out to side.

GET STRONG IN THE SHALLOW END

There are a number of strength and endurance moves you can do in the water, taking advantage of your natural buoyancy to elevate your heart rate and sculpt your legs and core. Perform these in a shallow portion of the pool

BICYCLE Lean back against the side of pool, with your arms outstretched at the edge. "Pedal" your legs at the surface.

PENDULUM SWING Lean back on the pool's edge with your arms resting on the sides. Extend your legs in front of you. Swing them over to the right, then to the left, keeping them together and underwater.

CRUNCH IN THE WATER Start as in the pendulum swing. Then extend your legs, feet together. Pull both knees into your chest. Return to the starting position.

FLUTTER KICK Hold on to the edge of the pool with your arms extended and body at water level; kick legs quickly.

GET THE BEST AQUA GEAR

Here are several handy helpers that might be perfect for your water workouts.

WATERPROOF FITNESS TRACKER A water proof fitness tracker allows you to time yourself in the pool as well as monitor your heart rate and calorie burn.

SUBMERSIBLE SNEAKERS These super light shoes dry quickly. They also offer nonslip soles and ankle support.

FOAM HAND BUOYS If you want to take your aerobic aquatics to the next level, try foam hand buoys (barbells), which range in size from 2.5 to 9 pounds (1–4 kg).

WEBBED GLOVES Emulate Aquaman with webbed gloves that increase resistance when your hands cut through the water.

GLOSSARY

aerobic Relating to activity that increases the body's demand for oxygen thereby resulting in temporary increase in breathing and heart rate.

anxiety A feeling of worry, nervousness, or unease.

circulation The movement of blood through the vessels of the body induced by the pumping action of the heart.

component A part or element of a larger whole.

depression A mood disorder marked by sadness and inactivity.

diabetes A disease in which the body's ability to produce or respond to the hormone insulin is impaired, resulting in abnormal metabolism of carbohydrates and elevated levels of glucose in the blood.

endurance The ability to sustain a prolonged stressful effort or activity.

exertion Physical or mental effort.

gait A manner of walking or moving on foot.

glucose A simple sugar that is an important energy source in living organisms and is a component of many carbohydrates.

incline A sloped or tilted surface.

metabolism The chemical changes in living cells by which energy is provided for vital processes and activities.

moderate Average in amount, intensity, or degree.

monitor To observe or check the progress of something over a period of time.

pulse The regular expansion of an artery caused by the ejection of blood by the contractions of the heart.

regimen A systematic plan to improve and maintain health.

resistance The power or capacity to resist, or push away.

respiration The action of breathing.

sedentary Not physically active.

stamina Staying power.

terrain The physical features of an area of land.

FURTHER READING

BOOKS

Ashwell, Ken. *The Student's Anatomy of Exercise Manual.* Hauppauge, NY: Barron's Educational Series, Incorporated, 2012.

Hutchinson, Alex. *Which Comes First, Cardio or Weights?: Fitness Myths, Training Truths, and Other Surprising Discoveries from the Science of Exercise.* New York, NY: Harper Collins Publishers, 2011.

Powers, Scott K., and Stephen L. Dodd. *Total Fitness and Wellness, the Mastering Health Edition.* London, UK: Pearson, 2016.

WEBSITES

Cardio Workouts
https://www.fitnessmagazine.com/workout/cardio/
Check out this one-stop webpage for a variety of cardio workouts.

Easy Exercises
https://kidshealth.org/en/teens/easy-exercises.html#catfit
Discover beginners cardio workouts with helpful pictures.

Fitness Planning
https://www.livestrong.com/article/232730-fitness-plan-for-teenagers/
Create your own fitness plan based on the helpful information on this informative webpage.

INDEX